Biographies of famous people to support
the National Curriculum.

Dick
Whittington

by Andrew Matthews
Illustrations by Lesley Bisseker

W
FRANKLIN WATTS
LONDON • NEW YORK • SYDNEY

First published in 1996 by
Franklin Watts
96 Leonard Street
London
EC2A 4RH

Franklin Watts Australia
14 Mars Road
Lane Cove
NSW 2066

This edition 1998

ISBN: 0 7496 2417 5

A CIP catalogue record for this book
is available from the British Library.

Dewey Decimal Classification Number: 361.7

10 9 8 7 6 5 4 3 2

Series editor: Sarah Ridley
Editor: Nicola Barber
Designer: Kirstie Billingham
Consultants: Dr Anne Millard and David Wray

Printed in Great Britain

Dick Whittington

Most people have heard of the legend of Dick Whittington and his cat. But not many people know that Dick Whittington was a real person. This is the true history of his life.

Dick Whittington was born in Pauntley in Gloucestershire around 1358. He was the youngest son of Sir William and Joan Whittington.

Sir William was poor, but he liked to live as if he was rich, so he borrowed money.
When he died in 1371, he left his family nothing but debts.

As the youngest son, Dick was expected to learn a trade. So, when Dick was only 13 he left home to live in London. There he became an apprentice to a mercer, a cloth merchant.

Goodbye, Dick and good luck!

The legend says that as Dick walked sadly away from Pauntley, he was followed by his pet cat.

London was nothing like
Pauntley. It was a huge place,
noisy and smelly, and the streets
were full of strangers.

Dick had to work very hard,
from early in the morning until
late at night.

Dick's master was a kind man and he taught Dick all he knew about where to buy cloth and wool, and how to treat his customers.

"You'll be a great mercer one day!" Dick's master told him, but Dick did not believe him.

Then, when he was 22, Dick's life changed. He met a young woman called Alice Fitzwarren, and they fell in love. Alice's father was Sir Ivo Fitzwarren.

Sir Ivo must have liked Dick, because he let the young lovers marry in 1380.

The legend about Dick and Alice is much more romantic! It tells of how Dick found a job as a kitchen boy in the house of Sir Ivo Fitzwarren. There, Dick met Alice.

Dick and Alice immediately fell in
love. But they could not get married
because Dick was too poor.

In real life, Sir Ivo was a wealthy landowner. *But in the legend of Dick Whittington he was a trader who owned many ships that sailed far across the seas.*

The legend says that Sir Ivo asked
his servants if they had anything they
wanted to sell abroad. Dick was so
poor that all he had was his pet cat.
He gave the cat to Sir Ivo.

*A year passed and Dick gave up hope
of being rich enough to marry Alice.
One Sunday morning he decided to go
home to his mother.*

But as he walked along, Dick heard
the church bells of London ringing.
They seemed to speak to him!

"Turn again, Whittington!
You worthy citizen
Turn again, Whittington!
Lord Mayor of London"

Dick ran back to Sir Ivo's house.
There he found a big box of gold and
jewels waiting for him. Where had
all this wealth come from?

Do you remember Dick's pet cat?
The legend says that she sailed far away
on one of Sir Ivo's ships to the land of
Barbary on the North African coast.

In the land of Barbary, the king's palace was full of rats and there were no cats to catch them. So the King of Barbary paid a fortune for Dick's pet cat.

This is the legend of how Dick Whittington became a rich man and married his beloved Alice.

In real life, Sir Ivo was so
pleased with his new son-in-law
that he gave him and his
daughter a lot of money as
a wedding present. Dick used
the money to start a business
of his own.

He bought good quality cloth from parts of Europe and the very best silks and velvets from China and India. He sold them to rich lords and ladies.

Dick was such a good salesman that his business grew. In 1395, he became Head of the Mercers' Company. This made him the most important cloth merchant in London.

Dick sold his richest gold cloth
to the King himself, King
Richard the Second of England.

Dick became so rich from his business that he began to lend money to King Richard.

The King was very grateful.
In 1397 he made Dick Whittington
Mayor of London. The bells in
the legend were right!

Richard the Second was an
unfortunate king who made
many enemies.

In 1399 Richard was forced to
give up the throne. He was put
into prison. A new king ruled
England, Henry the Fourth.

The new King had many
enemies and fought many battles.

King Henry needed money to
pay for his armies, and Dick
Whittington lent it to him.

When the King's daughters married, Dick sold them the cloth for their wedding dresses. Princess Blanche and Princess Philippa were delighted with their wonderful dresses!

At the age of forty-eight, Dick was
made Mayor of London again.

Henry the Fourth died in 1413,
and his son became Henry the
Fifth. The new King planned to
invade France. He asked Dick
Whittington for help, and Dick
lent him thousands of pounds.

Henry the Fifth beat the French
King at the battle of Agincourt
in 1415. After five more years
the fighting ended. In 1419,
Dick Whittington became Mayor
of London for the third time.

King Henry showed that he trusted Dick's honesty by putting him in charge of all the money that was used to repair Westminster Abbey.

Under Dick's direction, the Abbey was restored by the finest workmen in the land.

When Dick Whittington died
in 1423, at the age of sixty-five,
he was one of the richest men in
England. He had no children,
so he left most of his fortune to
help the people of London.

The money paid for a library,
so that students from poor
families could study.

Homes were built for old people and St Bartholomew's Hospital was repaired.

Wells were dug so that people would have fresh water to drink.

It's thanks to Dick Whittington that we've got such clean water...

After Dick Whittington died, people began to tell stories about him. They said that Dick once held a banquet, with King Henry and his Queen as guests of honour.

To keep them warm, Dick ordered the servants to throw on to the fire all the papers the King had signed when he borrowed money.

But the story people told most often was the legend of Dick Whittington and his cat.

No one knows if Dick Whittington ever really owned a cat or not, but a picture drawn some time after his death shows Dick wearing fine clothes. The Mayor's chain is around his neck, and he is stroking a cat.

Further Facts

At this time, London was a dirty
place. People threw sewage into a
gutter in the street. The gutters led
to a stream. Sometimes there was
so much sewage in
the streams that they
became blocked up.

Most merchants and craftsmen
belonged to a guild, or society. They
guarded the secrets of their trades

carefully. Guilds built halls to hold meetings and feasts. Most cities and large towns had at least one guild hall.

An apprentice agreed to work for his master for seven years, in exchange for learning a trade. Not all apprentices were as hard-working as Dick. Some played football in the street. When one street played against another, the game sometimes turned into a fight!

Important dates in
Dick Whittington's lifetime

1358   Dick Whittington born.

1371   Sir William Whittington dies.
Dick goes to London.

1380   Dick marries Alice Fitzwarren.

1395   Dick made Head of the Mercers' Company.

1397   Dick made Mayor of London.

1399   Richard II gives up the throne.
Henry IV becomes King.

1403   Henry IV wins the Battle of Shrewsbury.
War with France.

1406   Dick made Mayor of London again.

1413   Henry IV dies. Henry V becomes King.

1415   Henry V wins the Battle of Agincourt.

1419   Dick made Mayor of London for the
third time.

1420   War with France ends.

1422   Henry V dies. Henry VI becomes King
whilst still a baby.

1423   Dick Whittington dies.